A DAY IN THE LIFE OF A COMMUNITY SERVICE VEHICLE

A DAY IN THE LIFE OF A BUS

by Mae Respicio

PEBBLE
a capstone imprint

Published by Pebble, an imprint of Capstone
1710 Roe Crest Drive, North Mankato, Minnesota 56003
capstonepub.com

Library of Congress Cataloging-in-Publication Data is available on the Library of Congress website.
ISBN: 9780756586829 (hardcover)
ISBN: 9780756586775 (paperback)
ISBN: 9780756586782 (ebook PDF)

Summary: *Swish!* The bus door opens. People get on board, and the bus is off to its next stop. What equipment do these busy vehicles have? How is it used? Go behind the scenes to see what buses do to help in communities from sunrise to sunset.

Editorial Credits
Editor: Carrie Sheely; Designer: Elyse White; Media Researcher: Jo Miller; Production Specialist: Tori Abraham

Image Credits
Getty Images: Apriori1, 18, Drazen Zigic, 8, Hinterhaus Productions, 11, Jeremy Poland, 5, skynesher, 12, SolStock, 17; Shutterstock: Aleksandrs Samuilovs, 21 (plate), Art Konovalov, 16, hedgehog94, 19, inxti, 21 (pens) johan kusuma, 9, kozirsky, 20 (paints), LnP images, 10, MAHATHIR MOHD YASIN, 7, Mikbiz, cover (front and back), rawf8, 20 (scissors), Red Confidential, 13, Roman Zaiets, 15, Shyamalamuralinath, 20 (glue), Walter Cicchetti, 6, 14

Printed and bound in China. 6097

TABLE OF CONTENTS

Words in **bold** are in the glossary.

ON THE GO!

Honk! Look! A big colorful bus drives down the street. Buses are vehicles that help in our **communities**. Buses pick up and drop off people at places they need to go. Many buses help in big cities.

MORNING CHECKS

The sun comes up. Buses are on the roads early. People need to get to work, school, and other places.

Buses are usually kept at **depots**. Every morning, the buses are lined up. Bus drivers go to the depot. They find the bus they will drive for the day.

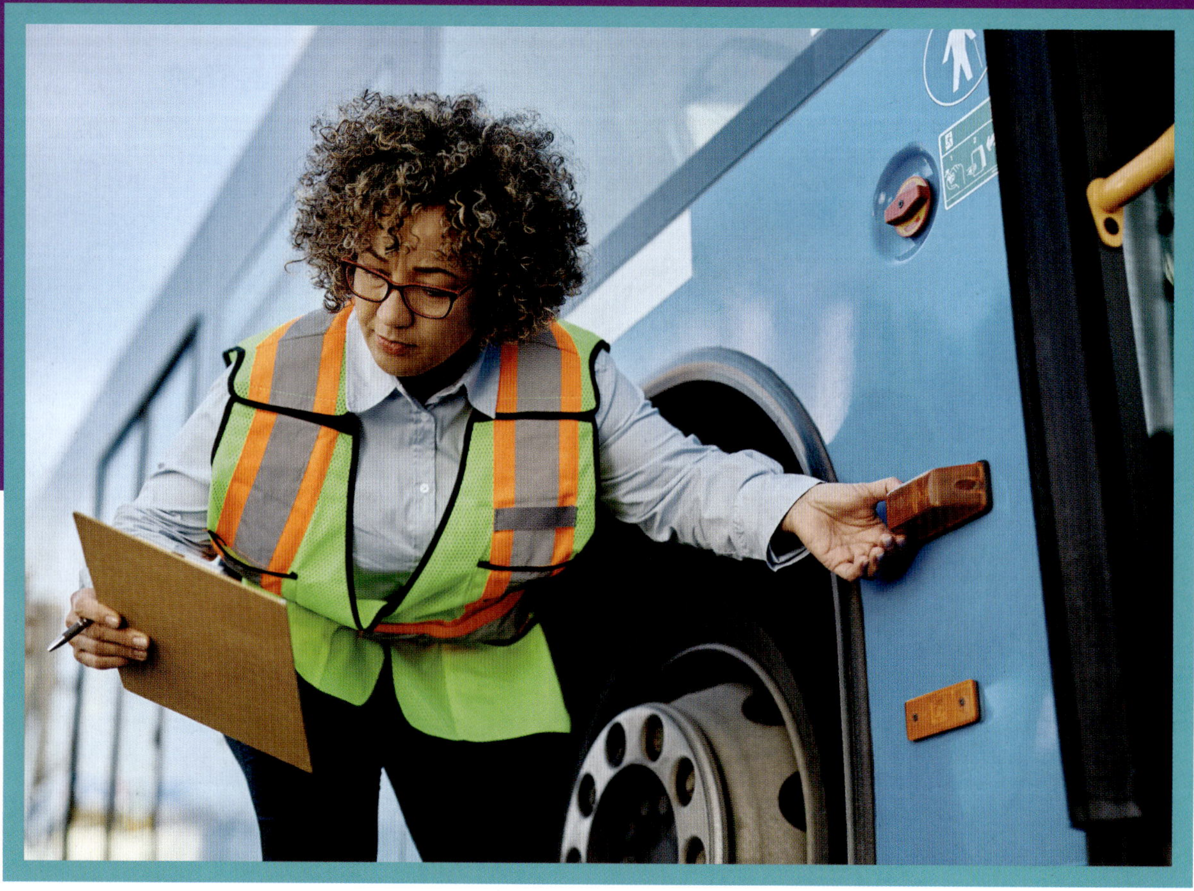

First, a driver checks the bus. Do the lights work? Are the tires in good condition? Is the bus clean inside? Yes!

Now the driver reviews the **route** and schedule. Finally, the driver starts the engine. Most bus engines run on **diesel fuel**. Some are powered by **natural gas**. Buses can be electric too.

The route lights up on the bus for people to see. Each bus also has a number. People can see which bus to take.

The bus slows. It makes its first stop of the day. *Whoosh!* The driver opens the door. **Passengers** get on the bus.

RIDING THE BUS

The bus has different places to sit. Seats can face the middle aisle or the bus's front. There's a special section for wheelchairs. On some buses, people can also stand. They hang onto handrails or grab bars.

Some buses have stop buttons or pull cords. Riders can use them right before their stop. The driver then knows someone needs to get off the bus.

WORK ALL DAY

The bus moves through heavy **traffic** downtown. *Phhsst!* The bus slows down. Why does it make that sound? Buses have air brakes. These brakes are lightweight and dependable.

At the next stop, someone in a wheelchair needs to board. The driver lowers the wheelchair ramp. The person goes up the ramp.

In the afternoon, there is a rainstorm. The driver turns on the windshield wipers. *Splash!* The bus goes through big puddles. The bus tires grip well even on wet roads.

The bus driver hears the **dispatcher** over the radio. She tells the bus driver there is a traffic accident on the route. The bus driver takes a different route.

SUNSET AT THE DEPOT

After the sun sets, the last riders get off. They wave goodbye to the driver. See you next time!

The bus heads back to the depot. It gets refueled. Then it's cleaned for the next trip. The workday is done. Tomorrow the bus will help again!

PAPER PLATE BUS

You've learned all about buses. Now you can make your own bus!

What You Need:

- paper plate
- scissors
- paints (at least two colors)
- glue or glue stick
- markers

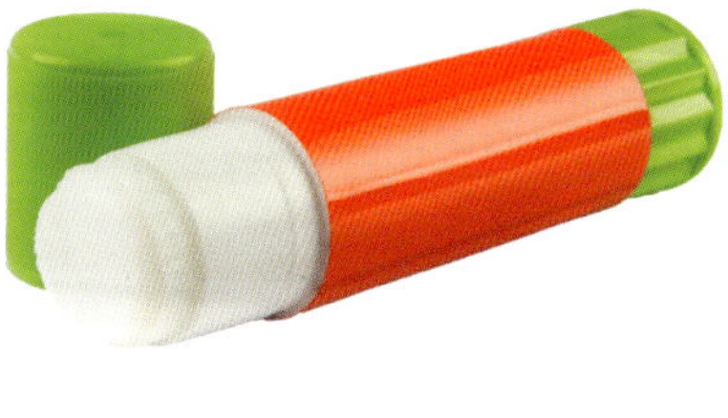

What You Do:

1. Cut the paper plate in half. Paint half of the plate in one color. Paint two circles on the other half of the plate in another color.
2. Carefully cut out the painted circles from the paper plate. Glue the circles to the cut end of the other half of the plate. These are the wheels.
3. Use the markers to draw windows on your bus. Then draw designs on your bus to make it your own. What number is your bus?
4. Share your bus with your family and friends.

GLOSSARY

community (kuh-MYOO-nuh-tee)—a group of people who live in the same area

depot (dee-POH)—a place that stores buses or other vehicles

diesel fuel (DEE-zuhl FYOOL)—a heavy oil that burns to make power

dispatcher (dis-PACH-uhr)—a person who plans bus routes and communicates information to bus drivers

fuel (FEW-ul)—anything that can be burned to give off energy

natural gas (NACH-ur-uhl GAS)—a gas made in the earth that can be burned

passenger (PASS-uhn-jur)—someone other than the driver who travels in a vehicle

route (ROUT)—the road or course followed to get somewhere

traffic (TRAF-ik)—the movement of cars, trucks, and buses on roads

READ MORE

Ackerman, Sara Holly. *Not Just the Driver!* San Diego: Beach Lane Books, 2024.

Beevor, Lucy. *Read All About Transportation.* North Mankato, MN: Capstone, 2022.

Dickmann, Nancy. *City Buses.* North Mankato, MN: Capstone, 2022.

INTERNET SITES

The Fact Site: 10 Bustling Facts About Buses
thefactsite.com/bus-facts

Kiddle: Public Transport Facts for Kids
kids.kiddle.co/Public_transport

PBS LearningMedia: What Is Transportation?
tpt.pbslearningmedia.org/resource/ad87bdb6-f349-4bdc-afa6-2446ab826eb2/what-is-transportation-young-explorers

INDEX

ABOUT THE AUTHOR

Mae Respicio is a nonfiction writer and award-winning author of novels including *How to Win a Slime War*. Mae lives with her family in California, and they love exploring new cities by bus.